PROSECUTING WAR CRIMES

Seeking Justice for the Victims of War

John Allen

ReferencePoint Press®

San Diego, CA

ReferencePoint Press®

About the Author
John Allen is a writer who lives in Oklahoma City.

Printed in the United States

For more information, contact:
ReferencePoint Press, Inc.
PO Box 27779
San Diego, CA 92198
www.ReferencePointPress.com

Picture Credits:
Cover: Drop of Light/Shutterstock.com
5: NurPhoto SRL/Alamy Stock Photo
10: Niday Picture Library/Alamy Stock Photo
12: Danvis Collection/Alamy Stock Photo
16: Everett Collection Historical/Alamy Stock Photo
20: Pictorial Press Ltd/Alamy Stock Photo
23: Associated Press
26: Shawhots/Alamy Stock Photo
31: Howard Sayer/Alamy Stock Photo
32: Associated Press
37: PORRO/SIPA/Newscom
40: Associated Press
43: Associated Press
45: ZUMA Press, Inc./Alamy Stock Photo
50: Frederic Legrand - COMEO/Shutterstock.com
52: Ukrinform/Alamy Stock Photo
55: American Photo Archive/Alamy Stock Photo

LIBRARY OF CONGRESS CATALOGING-IN-PUBLICATION DATA

Names: Allen, John, 1957- author.
Title: Prosecuting war crimes : seeking justice for the victims of war / John Allen.
Description: San Diego : ReferencePoint Press, 2023. | Includes bibliographical references and index.
Identifiers: LCCN 2023021364 (print) | LCCN 2023021365 (ebook) | ISBN 9781678207380 (library binding) | ISBN 9781678207397 (ebook)
Subjects: LCSH: War crimes (International law)--Juvenile literature. | War crime trials--Juvenile literature. | War victims--Legal status, laws, etc.--Juvenile literature. | War--Protection of civilians--Juvenile literature. | Combatants and noncombatants (International law)--Juvenile literature. | Prosecution--Juvenile literature. | Criminal procedure (International law)--Juvenile literature. | Restorative justice--Juvenile literature.
Classification: LCC KZ7145 .A945 2023 (print) | LCC KZ7145 (ebook) | DDC 341.6/9--dc23/eng/20230613
LC record available at https://lccn.loc.gov/2023021364
LC ebook record available at https://lccn.loc.gov/2023021365

CONTENTS

A Test for War Crimes Trials in Ukraine

In May 2022, a twenty-one-year-old Russian soldier became the first person tried for war crimes in Ukraine. Army sergeant Vadim Shishimarin was charged with the fatal shooting of an unarmed civilian in the first days of Russia's invasion of its neighboring country. The incident had occurred in February in the village of Chupakhivka, about 180 miles (290 km) east of Kyiv, Ukraine's capital. Investigators learned that Shishimarin and a group of Russian soldiers had stolen a car to flee the village after the breakdown of their armored vehicle. They spotted an elderly man speaking on his cell phone while walking his bike along a sidewalk. Afraid that the man might reveal their position, Shishimarin's colleagues wanted him silenced. The young sergeant aimed his automatic AK-47 rifle and fired, striking the man in the head and killing him.

Shishimarin's trial was viewed by many as a test of whether war crimes could be prosecuted fairly while the war raged in Ukraine. Baby-faced and slender in a blue and gray hoodie, Shishimarin shifted uneasily as he sat inside a protective glass box in a Kyiv courtroom. A series of witnesses and friends of the victim testified to the killing. Some could not contain their outrage, shouting at the young Russian and rejecting his defense that he was just following orders. Shishimarin apologized to the victim's widow and pleaded guilty. The judge sentenced him to life in prison. "Given that the crime committed is a crime against peace, security, humanity and the international legal order," said Judge Serhiy Agafonov, "the court does not see the possibility of imposing a (shorter) sentence."[1] Two months later, however, an appeals court reduced the sentence to fifteen years. Shishimarin's defense lawyer predicted he would soon be returned to Russia in a prisoner exchange.

Enforcing the Rules of War

The drive to prosecute war crimes is relatively new, dating back only to the mid-twentieth century. It emerged from efforts to set rules for warfare, as in the Hague Convention of 1907 and the later Geneva Conventions. These agreements aimed to provide

Russian soldier Vadim Shishimarin, charged with the shooting death of an unarmed Ukrainian civilian, appears at a 2022 court hearing. The trial was seen as a test of whether war crimes could be prosecuted fairly in the midst of war.

protections for civilians and other noncombatants during armed conflict. They offered guidelines on how armies should conduct themselves in warfare. Most important was the rule that military forces must distinguish between enemy combatants and civilians. Deliberately targeting civilians was expressly prohibited. Parties to a conflict were required to take every reasonable precaution to avoid civilian casualties.

After World War II, the Nuremberg Trials became the first international war crimes tribunal in history. Over nine months, twenty-four highly ranked military, political, and industrial leaders of Nazi Germany were indicted for war crimes, with twelve sentenced to death. Subsequent trials dealt with hundreds of other war criminals among the Nazis and their allies. One of the main objects of the Nuremberg Trials and other tribunals was to establish that Nazi Germany had committed what were called crimes against humanity. These included the crime of genocide against European Jews and other ethnic groups.

Nuremberg became a model for prosecuting war crimes decades later in the former Yugoslavia as well as in Bangladesh and Rwanda. Today, the International Criminal Court (ICC) in The Hague, located on the west coast of the Netherlands, prosecutes those accused of war crimes, crimes against humanity, and genocide. In its mission, the ICC receives the support of 123 countries worldwide. Some nations, including Russia and China, have not signed the United Nations (UN) treaty that governs the court and are not subject to its jurisdiction.

A Challenge to Prosecute

There was a swiftness and efficiency to the Shishimarin case that did not reflect how difficult it can be to prosecute offenders for war crimes while a conflict is ongoing. Gathering evidence and interviewing witnesses amid bloodshed and carnage can seem like a hopeless task. Many experts on war crimes also point out that convicting lower-level figures like Shishimarin does not address the perpetrators who are truly responsible. After all, it was Russian president Vladimir Putin who illegally sent Russian troops into southern Ukraine to seize Crimea in 2014. Likewise, his full-scale invasion of Ukraine in February 2022 was unprovoked. Yet unless Ukraine can win the war outright, it is unlikely that Putin or his generals will ever face a war crimes tribunal. "None of this would be happening if Russia had not invaded," says Philippe Sands, a specialist on international law. "The danger that we face is that in five years' time, we will have three or four trials of low-grade, useless sorts of characters that are totally irrelevant, and the top people just get off scot-free."[2]

> **"The volume of war crimes that we believe we are discovering in our daily work is overwhelming."[3]**
>
> —Christo Grozev, executive director of Bellingcat, a group that investigates war crimes

Nonetheless, there are plenty of dedicated people, both inside and outside of war zones, who continue to pursue the truth. Backed by a coalition of nations, they spend hours poring over evidence of war crimes on social media, in news articles, and via other outlets. Their hope is that by documenting the crimes and atrocities committed by ordinary troops, they will help bring leaders such as Putin to justice. "We are discovering the enormity of war for the first time in our lifetime in a way that is near us and a way that we can see it in social media," says Christo Grozev, executive director of Bellingcat, an investigative group based in the Netherlands. "And the volume of war crimes that we believe we are discovering in our daily work is overwhelming."[3]

CHAPTER ONE

The Geneva Conventions and the Laws of Modern Warfare

Just before midnight on October 1, 2022, someone uploaded a disturbing video to the social media app Telegram. It shows fifteen Azerbaijani soldiers rounding up a group of eight unarmed men wearing Armenian military garb. Halfway through the forty-second clip, a male voice repeatedly says, "Don't shoot!" But three of the Azerbaijanis have already begun firing their assault rifles at the seated Armenians. The close-range shootings last about twelve seconds, with a few bursts of fire afterward. Clearly, seven of the eight Armenian soldiers are killed, with the last perhaps clinging to life.

The next day a report on Twitter claimed that the execution-like shootings took place along Armenia's mountainous border with Azerbaijan, where territorial disputes have been ongoing for decades but flared up into armed conflict in 2022. Further investigation by Human Rights Watch and the Prosecutor General's Office of Azerbaijan determined that the incident had occurred about two weeks earlier and almost certainly constituted a war crime. The third Geneva Convention forbids the killing, mistreatment, or torture of prisoners of war (POWs). Yet war zones produce blatant violations like this one all too often. "These soldiers had been captured and laid down their arms," said Hugh Williamson, Human Rights Watch's Europe and Central Asia director. "Their captors had an obligation to treat them humanely, and instead it appears that Azerbaijani forces shot them in cold blood. Now they need to be held accountable."[4]

The First International Rules of War

The whole point of treaties such as the third Geneva Convention is to hold violators accountable for crimes committed in warfare. Both Azerbaijan and Armenia are parties to the four Geneva Conventions of 1949, as are 194 other countries. Although these agreements are difficult to enforce during a conflict, the authority to enforce them comes from the UN Security Council. In 2002, the UN created the ICC to prosecute war crimes like the alleged executions in Azerbaijan. And in this instance, Azerbaijan authorities have arrested suspected participants.

> "These [Armenian] soldiers had been captured and laid down their arms. Their captors had an obligation to treat them humanely, and instead it appears that Azerbaijani forces shot them in cold blood. Now they need to be held accountable."[4]
>
> —Hugh Williamson, Human Rights Watch's Europe and Central Asia director

The push to create rules of war goes back to the mid-nineteenth century. Before that, any such rules had been unwritten and haphazardly applied. But as military weapons became more destructive and armies aimed at total war, there were calls for certain guidelines to protect civilians and combatants alike. In 1863, at the height of America's Civil War, the Union army issued a handbook for its soldiers that became known as the Lieber Code. The name referred to Dr. Francis Lieber, a German-born history and political science professor at Columbia University who was chosen to draft the handbook. Signed by President Abraham Lincoln, the code included wartime laws and regulations to govern the army's conduct in the field. It had sections on protecting civilians, taking and holding POWs, and exchanging prisoners. The code stressed that all Confederate prisoners, including guerrilla fighters, should receive the same humanitarian treatment.

One year after the Lieber Code appeared in America, there emerged in Europe an even more important milestone for the rules of war. It began when Henri Dunant, a Swiss businessman, traveled to the Italian town of Solferino, where Napoleon III was leading his French troops in a bloody campaign against Austrian armies. Dunant hoped to meet with Napoleon III to secure water rights for his grain mill back home. Instead, he arrived to find terrible carnage and suffering. Thousands of dead and wounded soldiers lay in the fields. The French had only six doctors to treat more than nine thousand wounded men. They were also holding Austrian doctors as prisoners instead of letting them attend to the injured. Dunant did what he could to help care for the casualties. When he returned to his native Geneva, he wrote a piercing memoir about the scenes he had witnessed. He pro-

The Lieber Code, a handbook aimed at regulating conduct by Union army soldiers during the Civil War, included sections on the humanitarian treatment of civilians and Confederate prisoners (pictured).

The Rome Statute and the International Criminal Court

In July 1998, world diplomats adopted the Rome Statute, named for the conference's host city in Italy. The treaty set up the International Criminal Court (ICC)—also situated in The Hague—as the world's independent tribunal for war crimes, including crimes against humanity and genocide. It gave the ICC authority to investigate and prosecute alleged war crimes involving any of its 123 member nations, including crimes committed by their people or on their territory. The Rome Statute went into effect in 2002.

The United States helped to create the Rome Statute, but in 1998 the American delegation chose not to sign it. American experts in international law feared that the Rome Statute gave the ICC too much power and threatened to weaken American sovereignty. They warned it could leave American military or intelligence personnel vulnerable to prosecution for alleged crimes, such as torturing prisoners in Afghanistan. The Joe Biden administration has generally supported the ICC's mission and has cooperated with its investigations. However, it shows no sign of adopting the statute. "The United States played a pioneering role in creating the principles of international justice," says Adam Keith, director of Human Rights First, "though its leadership on that front since Nuremberg has been inconsistent, to say the least."

Adam Keith, "Justice for Ukraine and the U.S. Government's Anomalous Int'l Criminal Court Policy," Just Security, March 8, 2022. www.justsecurity.org.

posed setting up an international aid group for medical care during wartime. It would maintain stockpiles of emergency medical supplies to care for wounded soldiers on all sides. He also recommended that medical workers be given special legal protections as noncombatants. Dunant's proposals led to the formation of the International Committee for Relief to the Wounded. It was later renamed for its easy-to-identify symbol, becoming the International Committee of the Red Cross.

In 1864, representatives from sixteen European countries and several American states met in Dunant's home city to draft the first Geneva Convention on the rights of combatants. The convention focused on principles for the treatment of wounded soldiers during war. Casualties were to be cared for without regard to their nationality. Medical personnel were guaranteed protection as neutral figures. The distinctive sign of the Red Cross was

Representatives from Europe and America sign the first Geneva Convention, which focused on principles for the treatment of wounded soldiers during war.

adopted as a symbol of their neutrality. In 1901, Henri Dunant was honored for his role in creating the first Geneva Convention by receiving the first-ever Nobel Peace Prize.

Addressing How Wars Are Fought

In 1898, Czar Nicholas II of Russia initiated the next major evolution in the rules of war. He and his foreign minister, Mikhail Muravyov, were alarmed by the number of new and deadly weapons being introduced on the battlefields of Europe. To set limits on their use, Nicholas helped organize the first Hague Convention in the Netherlands. Twenty-six nations attended the conference, which began on May 18, 1899, the czar's birthday.

The first Hague Convention used America's Lieber Code as the basis of its agreements. Among its articles on weapons, it prohibited the launching of explosives from balloons, outlawed the use of projectiles to spread poison gas, and banned bullets that would expand or flatten in a victim's body. Inspired by a growing pacifist movement, the conference also declared that international disputes should preferably be resolved by peaceful means. To adjudicate disagreements, the convention established the Permanent Court of Arbitration, which consisted of judges selected from member nations. However, the court could not ensure an end to military conflict.

In 1907, forty-four nations gathered for the second Hague Convention. In the intervening years Russia had lost a major conflict with Japan, showing how quickly the world's balance of power could change. The second convention reflected the largely seaborne nature of the Russo-Japanese War. It dealt mainly with the rules of naval warfare, including the use of mines to target submarines, attacks on merchant ships, and the conversion of merchant ships to warships. The second Hague Convention, like the first, tried but failed to set up binding international courts that could settle disputes and prosecute war crimes.

The conference closed with an agreement to meet again in a few years. However, the outbreak of World War I in 1914 spoiled those plans. Moreover, the brutal war saw many of the Hague agreements almost ignored. For example, all the major participants in World War I used poison gas. In April 1915, Germany launched the first chemical attack on Allied soldiers during the battles around Ypres, Belgium. German munitions experts released tons of deadly chlorine gas from stationary cylinders buried in the ground. A deadly cloud formed and wafted into enemy lines, forcing French troops to withdraw after suffering over two thousand casualties. Subsequent gas attacks hit British and Canadian forces. "The next thing we heard was this sizzling," recalled British officer Martin Greener. "And then [we] saw this awful cloud coming over. A great yellow, greenish-yellow, cloud. . . . Nobody knew what to think, I mean we knew what it was. Well then of course you immediately began to choke."[5] German officials claimed the attack did not violate the Hague agreements because it did not come from *projectiles* filled with poison gas. "Did [the Germans] technically violate the Hague Convention?" asks Marion Dorsey, a history professor at the University of New Hampshire. "No. But did they violate the spirit of the ban? Absolutely."[6]

"Did [the Germans] technically violate the Hague Convention? No. But did they violate the spirit of the ban? Absolutely."[6]

—Marion Dorsey, history professor at the University of New Hampshire

After the war, public outrage about the use of chlorine gas, mustard gas, and similar agents led to a special Geneva Protocol to the Hague Conventions. It banned outright the use of all chemical and biological weapons.

Recognizing Genocide as a War Crime

In May 1915, Great Britain, France, and Russia jointly condemned the Ottoman Turkish government for the mass murder of its ethnic Armenian Christian population. They referred to the killings as "new crimes . . . against humanity and civilization."[7] The Turkish government's aim was to shore up Turkish Muslim control in the mountainous region of eastern Anatolia. The killings continued from spring 1915 through autumn 1916. Out of a population of about 1.5 million Armenians, at least 664,000 lost their lives in the slaughter. Experts today say the actual total may have approached 1.2 million deaths. However, most nations failed to hold the Ottoman Turks accountable. Only Britain, which stationed an army of occupation in Turkish lands, compelled the new Turkish government to bring some culprits to military trial. There was still no international court to prosecute war criminals.

Almost unimaginably, World War II, which erupted in 1939, outdid its predecessor in death and destruction. Nazi Germany, under the leadership of Chancellor Adolf Hitler, committed horrific acts of mass murder, including the systematic killing of European Jews by murder squads and in death camps. In 1944, Raphael Lemkin, a Polish-born lawyer and jurist, wrote a book describing the Nazi atrocities. In researching the book, Lemkin recalled the Ottoman Turks' slaughter of the Armenians. It led him to coin the term *genocide*. "By 'genocide' we mean the destruction of a nation or of an ethnic group," Lemkin explained in the book. "This new word, coined by the author to denote an old practice in

> "By 'genocide' we mean the destruction of a nation or of an ethnic group. This new word . . . is made from the ancient Greek word *genos* (race, tribe) and the Latin *cide* (killing)."[8]
>
> —Raphael Lemkin, Polish-born lawyer and jurist

The Blue Shield to Protect Cultural Property

A lesser-known protection against war crimes emerged from the Hague Convention of 1954. After the Nazis' widespread looting of art treasures and destruction of monuments and historic buildings during World War II, the convention set up safeguards for cultural property during wartime. Parties to the treaty agreed to refrain from bombing or shelling sites such as museums, libraries, archives, monuments, sculpture gardens, and religious structures containing important cultural artifacts. They adopted the symbol of a blue shield to identify sites that are protected from attack. Blue Shield International is considered the cultural equivalent of the Red Cross.

The Iraq War demonstrated the need for Blue Shield protections. Iraq is not a signatory of the Hague Conventions. On April 9, 2003, when American troops captured Baghdad, the city's Iraq Museum was left unguarded. A small boy slipped in a window and unlocked the building. People streamed inside to take what they could carry. At first, they focused on practical items such as tables, chairs, phones, and computers. But eventually looters made off with more than fifteen thousand priceless artworks and objects from antiquity. Since then, Blue Shield International has worked with military officials in the North Atlantic Treaty Organization and other groups to protect and preserve cultural heritage.

its modern development, is made from the ancient Greek word *genos* (race, tribe) and the Latin *cide* (killing)."[8]

After the war ended with the Allies' victory over Germany, Lemkin took part in the Nuremberg Trials, the first genuine attempt to prosecute war crimes using international law. The major Allied powers (the United States, the United Kingdom, France, and the Soviet Union) established the International Military Tribunal to prosecute individuals—not nations—for war crimes. Lemkin tried to get the American legal team to include genocide in its indictment of certain Nazi officials and officers for the systematic murder of European Jews. However, it was decided that genocide had yet to be declared a crime under international law and so could not be included in indictments. Also, around this time, Lemkin learned that forty-nine members of his own family had been murdered in the Holocaust. He became even more determined to get genocide recognized as a war crime internationally.

Lemkin's dogged effort to gather allies and lobby other countries finally paid off. The United Nations had been founded in 1945 to manage international relations, and Lemkin helped bring a resolution before the body. On December 9, 1948, the UN passed the Convention on the Prevention and Punishment of Genocide. It was the first human rights treaty approved by the UN.

Prosecuting Crimes Against Humanity

One of the key innovations to emerge from the Nuremberg Trials was the concept of crimes against humanity. Its intent, which built on ideas from the earlier Geneva Conventions, was to protect civilians in both peacetime and wartime, even when the threat came from their own governments. Prior to this change, a government's abuse of its own citizens, as with the Nazi annihilation campaign against German Jews, was beyond the reach of international law. It was considered separate from war-related crimes between nations. However, officials from European governments in exile, Allied diplomats, and journalist observers knew that Nazi crimes

Gas masks protect several US soldiers but one soldier without a mask suffers the effects of a poison gas attack during World War I. Hague Convention agreements to not use poison gas were ignored during the war.

against civilians could not be separated from Germany's war aims. With this in mind, the post-Nuremberg trials that the United States conducted in occupied Germany from 1946 to 1949 made sure to include the revolutionary idea of crimes against humanity.

The concept also played an important part in a new round of postwar Geneva Conventions. In 1949, four conventions were adopted into international law, covering protections for sick and wounded soldiers on land and sea, POWs, and civilians, including those in occupied territory. The fourth Geneva Convention, which dealt with civilians, drew upon the events of World War II and the disastrous lack of protections for ordinary citizens during wartime. The conventions included a common article that required humane treatment for all people held by enemy forces, which "specifically prohibits murder, mutilation, torture, cruel, humiliating and degrading treatment, the taking of hostages and unfair trial."[9]

Strengthening Protections for Civilians

During the 1970s there was discussion of revising the 1949 Geneva Conventions to address how the postwar world had changed. A polarizing Cold War and the threat from nuclear arms had replaced the fear of invading armies. Wars of liberation—or wars to gain or regain independence—were fought mostly within countries and featured guerrilla fighting and sabotage. Often so-called freedom fighters did not wear uniforms and hid among civilian populations. These tactics had to be considered when framing the new agreements.

In 1979 diplomats at the conference voted to add two new protocols to the existing Geneva Conventions. Both protocols stressed the suffering of civilians during wartime, including those who faced homes and businesses destroyed, families torn apart, schools closed, and difficulties in obtaining food and water. Protocol I held that wars of liberation would be considered the same as international conflicts, with both sides obligated to follow the laws of war. Protocol II laid out stringent protections for civilians caught up in civil wars inside nations. It was the first such agreement to apply international law to warfare within a nation's borders. The protocols prohibited soldiers from posing as civilians and outlawed indiscriminate attacks on civilian areas or vital infrastructure.

Skeptics questioned whether, once hostilities broke out, the new rules would do much to shield ordinary people from the endless terrors of modern warfare. However, the protocols, along with the earlier Geneva Conventions and Hague Conventions, demonstrated that nations could work together to create something new and promising: a system of international humanitarian law.

The Nuremberg Trials

Beginning in December 1946, the Doctors Trial at Nuremberg, Germany, revealed samples of the gruesome medical research conducted by Nazi physicians during World War II. In one project, doctors collected 112 Jewish prisoners who were being held in concentration camps. The inmates, both men and women, were chosen for facial and body characteristics that Nazi doctors considered to be typical of their race. The prisoners were photographed and examined in detail. Then they were put to death with poison gas at the Natzweiler-Struthof concentration camp. Afterward, their bodies were transferred to a medical facility in Strasbourg, Germany. Nazi researchers, led by Professor August Hirt, conducted anatomical tests on the bodies before defleshing them to create skeletons. The skeletons were to be displayed in a medical museum at Reich University in Strasbourg, to show the supposed inferiority of the Jewish race.

Germany fell to the Allies before the project could be completed. Hirt committed suicide in 1945 to avoid capture. But others faced a reckoning inside the courtroom at Nuremberg one year later. Dr. Wolfram Sievers was a Nazi colonel and director of the Institute for Military Scientific Research. It was Sievers who rounded up the 112 "specimens" and delivered them to Hirt and his staff. Dr. Rudolf Brandt worked with Hirt to plan and create the museum's skeleton exhibit. Sievers and Brandt, along with several other Nazi doctors and scientists, were found guilty of crimes against humanity. They were hanged on June 2, 1948, at Landsberg Prison in Bavaria. "Ironically," writes Jerry Bergman, who has researched the case, "none of the defendants evinced any remorse . . . and many defended their work as 'good science.'"[10] In a secret report to his Nazi boss that was read out in court, Sievers admitted that no signs of racial inferiority had been found.

A Determined Push for Postwar Justice

The conviction of Sievers, Brandt, and others on charges of war crimes marked a new milestone in international law. For the first time, perpetrators of wartime atrocities were made to answer for their crimes in a court of law. The Nuremberg Trials dealt with high-level German political officials, industrialists, and military officers who were accused of committing war crimes against enemy troops and civilians. Chief among their crimes was taking part in the systematic murder of 6 million European Jews and as

High-level political and military leaders of the Nazi regime listen to testimony during the Nuremberg Trials. The extent of Nazi war crimes during World War II led to a more determined push for postwar justice.

many as 5 million other civilians in what is known today as the Holocaust.

"The criminality of the German leaders and their associates does not consist solely of individual outrages, but represents the result of a systematic and planned reign of terror."[11]

—President Franklin D. Roosevelt's staff, at the meeting of Allied leaders at Yalta in 1945

The notion of trying leaders for war crimes had arisen before. At the end of World War I, there had been discussions among the Allies about prosecuting Wilhelm II, the German emperor, for his role in starting the hostilities. The postwar Treaty of Versailles even called for Wilhelm to be tried. However, the Netherlands, the nation to which Wilhelm had escaped after the war, refused to hand him over, and the controversy died.

The extent of Nazi war crimes during World War II led to a more determined push for postwar justice. The idea of conducting trials for war crimes came up during wartime meetings among the "Big Three" Allied leaders: American president Franklin D. Roosevelt, British prime minister Winston Churchill, and Russian general secretary Joseph Stalin. At first, Churchill favored summary executions for Nazi leaders without trials, but American officials convinced him that trials would be more effective. The agreement that the Allied leaders signed in February 1945 at Yalta, a resort city on Ukraine's coast, declared that Nazi war criminals would be found and placed on trial in a special international court. Added to the document was an analysis by Roosevelt's staff that laid out the scope of Nazi crimes:

> The criminality of the German leaders and their associates does not consist solely of individual outrages, but represents the result of a systematic and planned reign of terror within Germany, in the satellite Axis countries, and in the occupied countries of Europe. . . . It has been marked by mass murders, imprisonments, expulsions and deportations of populations; the starvation, torture and inhuman treatment of civilians . . . and, after initiation of "total" war, its prosecution with utter and ruthless disregard for the laws and customs of war.[11]

After the conference, Allied officials noted the vital importance of trying high-ranking Nazis. They believed the trials would have three main benefits. First, they would hold Nazi war criminals accountable for their terrible actions. Second, they would help deter future war crimes by demonstrating that perpetrators would be brought to justice. Third, and perhaps most important, the trials would document Nazi war crimes so that doubters, inside and outside Germany, could not claim that defendants were convicted without evidence. With public trials, German citizens would learn about their government's crimes in detail and hopefully come to realize their own responsibility for what had occurred.

Organizing the Historic Trials

On May 8, 1945, Harry S. Truman, who had assumed the presidency after Roosevelt's death in office, set about organizing America's role in the proposed trials. Truman appointed Robert H. Jackson, an associate Supreme Court justice, to serve as chief prosecutor for the United States. Jackson led representatives of the four Allied governments—the United States, Britain, France, and the Soviet Union—to sign the London Charter, which laid out the rules and procedures the trials would follow. On August 8, 1945, they created the International Military Tribunal. Each Allied nation also appointed its own judge and prosecution team.

The trials took place at the spacious Palace of Justice in Nuremberg, Germany. The Allies chose Nuremberg for its symbolic significance. The city had hosted the largest Nazi rallies and represented the seat of Nazi power. Its shattered landscape also bore witness to the war's vicious fighting. As Sidney Olsen reported in the May 14, 1945, issue of *Life* magazine (using the German form of the city's name), "Nürnberg, once a city symbolizing German culture, then Hitler's symbol of Nazi *Kultur,* is now no symbol of anything. Today Nürnberg looks like all the rest of the shells of cities, a great waste of broken bricks."[12]

The trials faced challenges from the beginning. Some critics, recalling how the efforts to punish Germany after World War I

The United States, Great Britain, France, and the Soviet Union each appointed a judge and prosecution team for the International Military Tribunal at Nuremberg. The four judges are pictured in this October 1945 photo.

had contributed to Hitler's rise, worried that the Nuremberg Trials could have similar results. Others questioned the Allies' authority to conduct such trials when their own brutal war tactics could be questioned. There were concerns that American and other Allied military personnel might be exposed to similar prosecutions. However, public opinion in the Allied nations overwhelmingly supported the trials.

A Moral Statement on International Law During Wartime

On October 18, 1945, the four chief prosecutors of the tribunal filed indictments against twenty-four major German war criminals and seven organizations. Among those indicted were such high-profile Nazis as Hermann Göring, party leader and chief of the German air force; Joachin von Ribbentrop, who served as Hitler's foreign minister; and Rudolf Hess, Hitler's deputy and right-hand man. Prosecutors wanted to focus the first trial on German figures whom the public would recognize from news reports. Hitler, the head of the Nazi Party who had made himself

The Tokyo Trials

On May 3, 1946, a separate tribunal began its prosecution of Japanese war criminals in Tokyo, Japan. With the United States governing Japan after its surrender, the trials were orchestrated by General Douglas MacArthur in his role as supreme commander. The Allies created three broad categories of war crimes for the trials. Class A charges included crimes against humanity and were leveled against Japan's top political and military leaders. Class B and C charges were brought against Japanese of lower rank who were accused of conventional war crimes. To try the defendants, MacArthur set up the International Military Tribunal for the Far East with remarkable speed.

The trials lasted two and half years. All twenty-five defendants were found guilty of various war crimes and crimes against humanity, with seven of them sentenced to death. General Hideki Tojo, Japan's supreme commander in the war, tried to commit suicide before he could be executed, but American doctors were able to revive him. MacArthur refused to allow the hangings to be filmed or photographed. He also defended the procedure against criticisms of so-called victor's justice. "No human decision is infallible," he said, "but I can conceive of no judicial process where greater safeguard was made to evolve justice."

Quoted in *American Experience*, "The Tokyo War Crimes Trials," PBS. www.pbs.org.

the German dictator, could not be tried, having committed suicide at the war's end.

Jackson, the chief American prosecutor, opened the second day of the trial with a lengthy speech laying out its purpose. It was widely regarded as one of the great moral statements on international law and human rights. Jackson had spent the past several months on leave of absence from the US Supreme Court. Besides working on the London Charter, he had researched legal precedents for prosecuting war criminals and used them to prepare his opening statement. His tone was calm and serious as he explained to a hushed courtroom why this Nuremberg trial was so momentous:

> The privilege of opening the first trial in history for crimes against the peace of the world imposes a grave responsibility. The wrongs which we seek to condemn and punish have been so calculated, so malignant, and so devastating, that civilization cannot tolerate their being

ignored, because it cannot survive their being repeated. . . . What makes this inquest significant is that these prisoners represent sinister influences that will lurk in the world long after their bodies have returned to dust. We will show them to be living symbols of racial hatreds, of terrorism and violence, and of the arrogance and cruelty of power.[13]

Jackson admitted that the tribunal was new and even experimental, but he insisted that it would be carried out with the utmost sense of fairness and justice. Civilization could not make war impossible, he said, but it could put the force of international law on the side of peace.

Presenting Powerful Evidence of War Crimes

Following Jackson's opening speech, the trial would continue for the next 293 days. Instead of a single judge and jury, the trial featured a panel of four judges, one from each Allied nation. Participants wore headphones to hear translations of whatever was said in court. As Jackson promised, he and the other Allied prosecutors did not seek to convict the Nazi defendants on the testimony of their wartime enemies. In fact, they decided to limit eyewitness testimony, fearing that it would become too emotional and volatile for the courtroom. Instead, they offered evidence of war crimes based on the Nazis' own files, records, memos, photographs, and personal writings. However, some items entered into evidence did indeed make an emotional case. Among them was the shrunken head of a Polish Jew. The wife of the commandant at Buchenwald concentration camp had used it as a paperweight.

> **"The privilege of opening the first trial in history for crimes against the peace of the world imposes a grave responsibility. The wrongs which we seek to condemn and punish have been so calculated, so malignant, and so devastating, that civilization cannot tolerate their being ignored."[13]**
>
> —Robert H. Jackson, chief American prosecutor at the Nuremberg Trials

One of the most powerful pieces of evidence was presented on the trial's eighth day. It was a film of the Nazi death camps. The film was assembled from motion pictures shot by military photographers who entered the camps alongside the Allies' liberating armies. Details in the narration were drawn from the photographers' notes. The images of skeletal, half-dead inmates and piles of discarded corpses drew gasps from the courtroom. Defendants in the dock fidgeted, changed their seats, or tried to look away.

Defense attorneys argued that the accused had only been following orders and could not have acted otherwise. This ploy became known as "the Nuremberg Defense." "I don't see how they can fail to recognize a soldier's obligation to obey orders," said Alfred Jodl, chief of operations for the German High Command. "That's the code I've lived by all my life."[14] Nonetheless, according to rules set before the trial began, this defense would not relieve the accused of criminal liability but only potentially lessen their punishment. At any rate, the defendants showed little remorse in their testimony.

On March 18, 1946, three months into the proceedings, Jackson began the long-awaited cross-examination of Göring, the man designated as Hitler's successor. News reports described Göring as slippery in his responses. Time and again he would ask for Jackson's questions to be repeated or retranslated, ap-

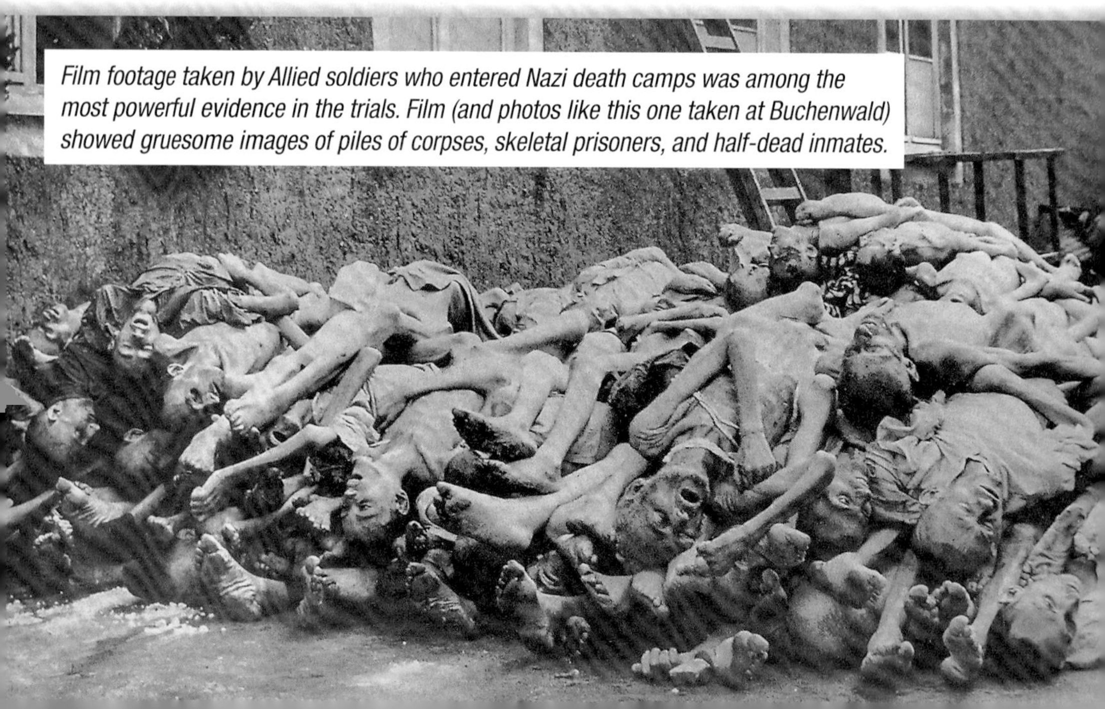

Film footage taken by Allied soldiers who entered Nazi death camps was among the most powerful evidence in the trials. Film (and photos like this one taken at Buchenwald) showed gruesome images of piles of corpses, skeletal prisoners, and half-dead inmates.

The Trial of Eichmann

Long after the Nuremberg Trials, agents in Israel continued to pursue Nazi war criminals. In May 1960 Mossad intelligence officers arrested Adolf Eichmann in Buenos Aires, Argentina, where he worked at a Mercedes-Benz factory. Eichmann remained the most notorious living Nazi to have escaped capture. He was instrumental in planning and implementing the Holocaust. During the war, he was brutally efficient in his management of the deportation of Jews to the death camps. He had also arranged for Jews' property to be seized and financial assets confiscated.

Eichmann's trial was conducted in the spirit of Nuremberg. A special tribunal of the Jerusalem District Court heard witnesses testify to Eichmann's role in the systematic mass murder of Europe's Jews. In his own defense, Eichmann resorted to the familiar claim that he was only a cog in the Nazi machinery. "There is a need to draw a line between the leaders responsible and the people like me," he wrote to Israel's president. "I was not a responsible leader, and as such do not feel myself guilty." Nonetheless, the court convicted Eichmann on all counts. On June 1, 1962, he was executed by hanging. He was then cremated, and his ashes were scattered in the sea, well beyond Israel's territorial waters.

Quoted in Catherine Farmer, "'They Were Just Following Orders,'" Centre for Holocaust Education, University College London, January 27, 2021. www.ucl.ac.uk.

parently to give himself a chance to think of an answer. He suggested that guilt for Nazi crimes lay exclusively with Hitler and his top conspirators, not with the Nazi Party. However, Jackson warned that Göring's testimony had a sinister motive. "I trust the Court is not unaware that outside of this courtroom is a great social question of the revival of Nazism," Jackson said, "and that one of the purposes of the Defendant Goering—I think he would be the first to admit—is to revive and perpetuate it by propaganda from this trial now in progress."[15] Jackson went on to show how Göring himself had authorized the seizure of Jewish businesses and property and the use of Jews as slave labor. His policies had set the stage for the death camps by denying the Jews' humanity. Confronted with his crimes, Göring trembled and became defiant.

Verdicts, Punishment, and Further Trials

Several months later, on October 1, 1946, the Nuremberg court issued its verdicts. Of the twenty-two defendants (two having been removed due to suicide or illness), nineteen were convicted and twelve were sentenced to death. Three of those convicted received a sentence of life imprisonment, with four others sentenced to prison terms of ten to twenty years. Three defendants were acquitted.

Hermann Göring committed suicide by taking a cyanide pill the night before his scheduled execution. The death sentences were carried out on October 16 by hanging the defendants one by one inside a gymnasium attached to the courthouse. Arthur Seyss-Inquart, an Austrian chancellor who oversaw the murders of more than half of the Netherland's Jews, was the last to be hanged. "I hope that this execution will be the last act of the tragedy of the Second World War,"[16] he said as the rope was placed around his neck.

"In the interests of peace and in order to protect mankind against future wars, it will be of decisive significance to have the principles which were employed in the Nuremberg trials . . . made a permanent part of the body of international law as quickly as possible."[17]

—Trygve Lie, the UN's first secretary-general

But twelve more Nuremberg trials took place between 1946 and 1949. Nearly two hundred Nazi defendants were executed in the subsequent trials, including doctors, lawyers, judges, military officers, and death camp commandants. Due to Cold War tensions with the Soviet Union, the United States conducted the later trials itself.

The Nuremberg Trials established a crucial benchmark for international law by prosecuting government and military officials for war crimes. Rather than hold theatrical show trials, the Allies focused on the solemn business of documenting the Nazi regime's heinous crimes. The success of the trials led the UN to endorse their principles. "In the interests of peace and in order to protect mankind against future wars," said Norway's Trygve Lie, the UN's first secretary-general, "it will be of decisive significance to have the principles which were employed in the Nuremberg trials . . . made a permanent part of the body of international law as quickly as possible."[17]

CHAPTER THREE

Prosecuting War Crimes in the Former Yugoslavia

Pursuit of war criminals can continue even after war crimes tribunals have been officially closed. In January 2023, a Serbian sausage maker living in a Cleveland, Ohio, suburb was indicted for making false statements on his application to become a US resident. According to a Justice Department filing, fifty-five-year-old Jugoslav Vidic claimed never to have participated in killing a person because of ethnic origin or political opinion. But in 1998 Vidic, a lieutenant in the breakaway Serb Army operating inside Croatia, had been convicted of murder by a Croatian court. The crime allegedly took place after Serbian forces attacked a meat-processing plant in Croatia. Vidic was observed leading a former coworker out of the plant at gunpoint. The coworker later was found dead, one of several Croat victims exhumed from a mass grave.

Vidic escaped to the United States, where he claimed special status as a war refugee. Instead of serving a twenty-year prison sentence in Croatia, he had spent twenty years living in America and running an ethnic sausage market. The war in the former Yugoslavia had ended years earlier, and a tribunal to prosecute its war criminals had shut down in 2017. Yet Vidic and others like him still face a possible reckoning for their past crimes. If convicted of falsifying his green card

> "[Vidic is] a war criminal and lied about that to the [Federal Bureau of Investigation], and we believe if he's out on bond, he'll flee. It's not just this case, but he's facing certain incarceration in Croatia."[18]
>
> —Jerome Teresinski, assistant US attorney

application and lying to federal investigators, Vidic faces a maximum sentence of fifteen years in prison. "He's a war criminal and lied about that to the [Federal Bureau of Investigation], and we believe if he's out on bond, he'll flee," said Assistant US Attorney Jerome Teresinski. "It's not just this case, but he's facing certain incarceration in Croatia."[18]

A Breakup Leads to Violent Change

During the early 1990s, the breakup of the Soviet Union led to rapid changes in Eastern Europe. Some countries enjoyed new freedoms that they had scarcely hoped for. But in other regions, the breakup let loose the twin furies of ethnic hatred and violence. The nation of Yugoslavia fell apart, with new states forming along ethnic lines. The result was years of especially vicious civil war. For example, Croatia declared its independence in 1991, only to have ethnic Serbs living in Croatia, such as Jugoslav Vidic, take up arms to establish their own state. People who had lived together for decades suddenly found themselves at one another's throats. Vidic had seen his former coworker at a rally shaking hands with Croatia's president, Franjo Tudjman, whom Vidic considered to be anti-Serbian. It was enough to make him target his former colleague.

Ethnic hatreds were inflamed with religious strife among Orthodox Christian Serbs; Bosniaks, or Muslim Bosnians; and Catholic Croats. This, combined with a crumbling economy, sparked conflict. As militias clashed across what once was Yugoslavia, Eastern Europe experienced its worst outbreak of violence since World War II. Much of the killing occurred in the war over Bosnia and Herzegovina and other breakaway republics. From 1992 to 1995, more than one hundred thousand people lost their lives in the Bosnian War. Civilians could not escape the chaos. The Bosnian Missing Persons Institute has estimated that thirty-two thousand civilians disappeared during the war.

Some of the worst violence took place toward the war's end in 1995. By that time, the remaining Muslims in Bosnia had taken refuge in three mountain towns in the east. The UN declared Srebrenica, the largest of the towns, to be a safe zone, under the protection of UN troops and North Atlantic Treaty Organization (NATO) peacekeeping forces. Nonetheless, Serbian troops proceeded to carry out a massacre of Bosnian Muslims in Srebrenica to rival the worst Nazi atrocities. It was estimated that more than eight thousand people were murdered. Men and boys were separated from women and young children and marched into the forest or taken to isolated fields. Many of the victims were forced to dig their own graves before being shot. "It sounds good—'safe areas,'" an American military officer serving in NATO told the *New York Times.* However, the peacekeepers, he said, "were little more than observers. They didn't have the firepower. The truth is the safe areas were always a myth."[19]

More than one hundred thousand people died in the Bosnian War. A crowded cemetery in Sarajevo is a reminder of the ethnic and religious hatred that fueled the war.

A New International Criminal Tribunal

Massacres like the one in Srebrenica—though often on a smaller scale—took place almost from the war's beginning. The stage was set when Croatia declared its independence in 1991, only to have Serbians in Croatia rebel to establish their own state. One year later, the new nation of Bosnia declared its independence and quickly received international recognition. Ethnic Serbs inside Bosnia rejected this move as well. Serbian forces set about to systematically remove Bosniaks from Bosnian territory, an operation that was labeled *ethnic cleansing*—another name for genocide. The Serbs, led by President Slobodan Milosevic, used military hardware from stockpiles in the former Yugoslavia to attack the Muslim enclaves. They surrounded the capital city of Sarajevo and drove the Bosniaks into detention camps where they were starved, tortured, and brutalized.

Reports of atrocities, emerging first in Croatia and months later in Bosnia, prompted the UN to act. In late 1992 a UN Commission of Experts visited the war-torn Balkans to investigate. The

The United Nations evacuates more than two thousand people from the besieged Muslim enclave of Srebrenica in 1993. Serbian forces slaughtered thousands of Muslim men and boys—actions later described as genocide.

Prosecuting Sexual Assault as a War Crime

In June 1998 a Bosnian Croat commander became the first person to be tried exclusively for sexual violence as a war crime. Anto Furundzija, leader of a paramilitary unit called the Jokers, had directed an assistant to rape a young Bosniak woman repeatedly during her interrogation. Although he did not commit the acts himself, Furundzija was found guilty as a coperpetrator. The tribunal's verdict was upheld on appeal, and Furundzija was sentenced to ten years in prison.

One of the International Criminal Tribunal for the former Yugoslavia's (ICTY's) most important additions to international law was to investigate and prosecute sexual assault as a war crime. Whereas violent sexual behavior had once been shrugged off as typical of soldiers in wartime, the tribunal recognized it as an aggressive tool of war, used to intimidate and terrorize enemy civilians. Authorities estimate that fifty thousand rapes occurred during the war. In some cases, where women were held captive and forced to comply with their captors' demands, including sexual demands, the defendants were also found guilty of enslavement. Victims who testified about sexual assault had their identities protected by appearing in closed session or with voice distortion on video feeds. Altogether the court convicted thirty-two individuals for crimes of sexual violence, representing about one-third of the total convictions.

commission documented war crimes ranging from ethnic cleansing of opposition groups to sexual assault and rape in detention camps to torture and murder of captured enemy soldiers. In addition, hundreds of thousands of civilians had been expelled from their homes and were facing an uncertain future.

With violations of the Geneva Conventions taking place almost daily, the UN Security Council created a new tribunal to address the mounting war crimes. In May 1993 the newly established International Criminal Tribunal for the former Yugoslavia (ICTY) aimed to prosecute those who organized, planned, and carried out the most serious offenses. The court consisted of sixteen permanent judges, chosen from the elite legal ranks in their home countries.

The ICTY faced several challenges in dealing with the numerous and often undocumented crimes in the Balkan conflict. Unlike the prosecutors in the Nuremberg Trials, it began to investigate war crimes while the fighting was still in progress. UN peacekeeping troops could not guarantee the safety of ICTY personnel as they sought to interview survivors and victims. The warring sides

"When I arrived at the ICTY on 15 August 1994 it was really against the ropes. The judges were embarrassed and extremely anxious and frustrated. . . . In effect, the ICTY had been written off by the politicians and the media."[20]

—Richard Goldstone, the ICTY's first chief prosecutor

commonly refused to grant investigators access to witnesses or alleged crime scenes. From the outset, the ICTY had limited resources to bring offenders to justice. "When I arrived at the ICTY on 15 August 1994 it was really against the ropes," recalls South African judge Richard Goldstone, the ICTY's first chief prosecutor. "The judges were embarrassed and extremely anxious and frustrated. There was only a skeleton staff. In effect, the ICTY had been written off by the politicians and the media."[20] In 1995, when a brokered peace deal ended the fighting, the ICTY swore to continue its pursuit of war crimes. But NATO officials, while voicing support for the tribunal's goals, declined to arrest indicted war criminals. They considered such efforts to be so-called mission creep, extending beyond their original task of peacekeeping. Skeptics declared that the ICTY was merely a salve for the West's conscience and was doomed to failure. Those responsible for the atrocities, including Serbia's President Milosevic and Bosnian Serb leaders Radovan Karadzic and Ratko Mladic, ignored the ICTY altogether.

A Hunt for War Criminals

Despite these reactions, the ICTY redoubled its efforts. A Canadian judge named Louise Arbour, who replaced Goldstone as chief prosecutor, pressured NATO's member states into finally helping to hunt down alleged war criminals in the Balkans, albeit reluctantly. Arbour threatened to organize her own special weapons and tactics team if NATO commanders continued to resist. NATO relented and provided strike teams to locate and capture suspects. The first arrests took place on July 10, 1997, as part of Operation Tango. After a lengthy stakeout hidden in a lakeside trench, a British special forces unit arrested key officials in the Bosnian town of Prijedor. The officials, including Prijedor's mayor and sheriff, had helped round up the town's Muslims for transport

Capturing Europe's Most Wanted War Criminal

In July 2008, security officers in Serbia arrested Radovan Karadzic, the most wanted person in Europe. The arrest capped a thirteen-year manhunt conducted by military and law enforcement agencies worldwide. Karadzic was a Serbian warlord responsible for horrific war crimes, including the 1995 mass murder of eight thousand Bosniaks in Srebrenica. Following his indictment that year, Karadzic lived openly in the mountain village of Pale outside Sarajevo. He was convinced that UN peacekeepers were not inclined to arrest former Serb officials.

Only in 1997, when the Bill Clinton administration made Karadzic's capture a priority, did he slip into hiding. Karadzic grew a bushy white beard and pretended to be Dragan Dabic, a mystic healer and expert on herbal medicine. Sympathetic agents in Serbia's intelligence service helped him establish this new identity. As Dabic, he became a star in the Serbian alternative medicine market. In 2008, his scheme faltered when his brother called him on a phone line monitored by the Central Intelligence Agency. He was soon arrested on a street in Belgrade. "At 9.30 pm on 18 July 2008, the flamboyant fiction that had been Dragan David Dabic evaporated," writes investigative journalist Julian Borger. "In his place, the ghost of Radovan Karadzic . . . rematerialized on a Belgrade roadside."

Julian Borger, "The Hunt for Radovan Karadzic, Ruthless Warlord Turned 'Spiritual Healer,'" *The Guardian,* March 22, 2016. www.theguardian.com.

to concentration camps, where many of the inmates died from beatings or starvation.

Over the next several years, the NATO powers engaged in a massive manhunt. Tactics ranged from sting operations to military assaults by helicopter. To capture a suspect named Stevan Todorovic, a team tracked him to his log cabin hideout deep within a Serbian forest. Bound and hooded, Todorovic was driven to the Drina River, then motored across into Bosnia in a rubber boat. Eventually he was extradited to the ICTY at the Hague. Todorovic, a Bosnian Serb and former police chief who had persecuted and tortured non-Serbian civilians, was one of 161 war criminals to be indicted and put on trial.

For some, the NATO dragnet seemed to lack the needed urgency. "We are pleased that at the end of the day [the accused] were all arrested, but was it really necessary that it took so long, and was so painful?" said Belgian jurist Serge Brammertz, who became the ICTY's chief prosecutor in 2008. "Many of the survivors of the crimes in the meantime died without seeing justice being done. So I share the frustration."[21]

Trials Marked by Delays and Slow Proceedings

Delays and procedural issues also marred the trials of some of the most notorious defendants in the Balkan war. For example, Arbour issued an arrest warrant for Milosevic, the former president of Serbia, in May 1999, yet the newly elected Serbian government did not hand him over to the tribunal until June 2001. Milosevic's trial finally got under way on February 12, 2002. For the first time in history, a head of state was facing prosecution for war crimes. Several indictments focused on Milosevic's efforts to remove Albanians by force from the Serbian province of Kosovo. He allegedly ordered a systematic campaign of terror and violence, including murder, torture, and looting, to deport more than eight hundred thousand Albanians. He was also accused of genocide and crimes against humanity in Croatia. His troops murdered hundreds of Croats and other non-Serb individuals; imprisoned, tortured, and sexually assaulted thousands more; and demolished Croat homes and cultural monuments. He was charged with similar crimes connected with removals and forcible detentions in Bosnia and Herzegovina.

The judges were determined to respect Milosevic's rights as a defendant, while a stream of live witnesses and written testimony accused him of dozens of war crimes in three different countries over ten years. The prosecution contended that Milosevic's victims numbered in the tens of thousands. Such a mass of information took months to present. Serving as his own defense lawyer, Milosevic was given plenty of time to review the testimony and cross-examine witnesses. His poor health, including a history of heart disease, diabetes, and hypertension, also caused delays. He was unable to appear in court for weeks at a time.

Former Serbian president Slobodan Milosevic appears before a war crimes tribunal in 2002. His trial marked the first time in history that a head of state faced prosecution for war crimes.

In the end, the ICTY reached no decision in the case. On March 11, 2006, more than four years after the trial began, Milosevic died from a heart attack in his prison cell at age sixty-four. The court's verdict was only a few weeks away. Relatives of his victims felt cheated that he had escaped judgment for his crimes. "In death as in life, Slobodan Milosevic, the 'butcher of the Balkans. . . ,' created bitter division," wrote *The Guardian*'s Peter Beaumont. "His death is a crushing blow to the tribunal and to those who wanted to establish an authoritative historical record of the Balkan wars."[22]

Justice for other high-profile perpetrators met with even longer delays. It took until March 2016—more than two decades after the war began—to convict Bosnian Serb leader Karadzic of crimes against humanity and genocide. His original sentence of forty years was later increased to life imprisonment. In 2017, Bosnian Serb military commander Mladic also received a life sentence for war crimes and genocide. Mladic's conviction for genocide was linked to his role in the 1995 massacre of eight thousand Bosniaks in Srebrenica.

A War That Will Not Go Away

For people in the Balkans, reminders of the war are not hard to find. This includes tributes to war criminals. In the Serb-dominated half of Bosnia, giant posters of Mladic are displayed in public squares. A student dorm is named for Karadzic. In July 2022 the Missing Persons Institute of Bosnia and Herzegovina announced that the skeletal remains of thousands of Bosniak victims had been found in eighty-five separate mass graves. The grim findings attest to the 1995 genocide that Bosnian Serb forces carried out in Srebrenica.

Yet these reminders show the importance of the ICTY trials. For the first time, investigators had gathered evidence of war crimes while a conflict was in progress. The Balkan tribunal also was the first to prosecute sexual assault as a war crime. It inspired other courts to deal with war crimes in Rwanda, Sierra Leone, and Cambodia. For all their difficulties and delays, the ICTY's Balkan trials changed public attitudes. "When I was in law school, it was normal for dictators to retire in the south of France," says Diane Orentlicher, a law professor at American University in Washington, DC. "All my students have grown up in a world where it's normal to think a mastermind of atrocities must be brought to book."[23]

"All my students have grown up in a world where it's normal to think a mastermind of atrocities must be brought to book."[23]

—Diane Orentlicher, law professor at American University

CHAPTER FOUR

Confronting War Crimes in Syria

Bringing war criminals to justice often depends on unusual circumstances. In January 2022, a court in Koblenz, Germany, convicted a former colonel in Syria's secret police of war crimes and crimes against humanity. In 2011, as the rumblings of civil war began in Syria, Anwar Raslan had overseen the torture, sexual assault, and murder of political prisoners at Al-Khatib, one of that nation's most notorious detention centers. Prisoners were packed into sweltering cells. They received beatings and electric shocks and were forced to drink from toilets. Raslan was found guilty of torturing at least four thousand detainees and murdering fifty-eight.

Ironically, Raslan had later turned against the repressive Syrian government of Bashar al-Assad. In 2014, after his hometown was attacked by government forces, he joined the opposition and then fled to Germany. He applied for asylum in that country and lived there peacefully for several years. In 2019, however, reports from witnesses among the eight hundred thousand Syrian refugees in Germany led to Raslan's arrest. Evidence presented at his trial included eyewitness accounts of torture as well as photographs of dead prisoners that were smuggled out of Syria. Former prisoners and the relatives of victims praised the court for following through on a difficult prosecution. Legal experts said the verdict sent a strong message that war crimes would not go unpunished. They also noted the milestone of targeting

Anwar Raslan (foreground), a former colonel in Syria's secret police, appears in a German courtroom in 2022. He was convicted of war crimes in connection with the torture and murder of political prisoners.

a government that remains in power. "This was a very important verdict," says Stefanie Bock, the director of the International Research and Documentation Center for War Crimes Trials at the University of Marburg in Germany. "The signal is: There is no safe haven for war criminals. It's a clear sign that the world will not stand by and do nothing."[24]

Rebelling Against a Brutal Regime

In Syria, where the bloody civil war continues, Raslan's trial made little difference. The Assad regime that holds the country in its grip goes back five decades. Hafez al-Assad seized power via a coup in 1971 and ruled with an iron fist until his death in 2000. His son Bashar, a soft-spoken eye doctor who had been living in London, replaced him as president. For a time, Syrians held out hope that the westernized younger Assad would restrain the secret police and allow the people more political freedom. However, such hopes were soon dashed. In 2011, when the so-called Arab Spring saw freedom movements erupt across the Middle East and North Africa, toppling dictators with shocking suddenness, Assad and his lieutenants cracked down with all the ferocity of his father.

The fuse of rebellion in Syria was lit by a schoolboy's modest act of defiance. In Daraa, a run-down village on the southern border, fourteen-year-old Mouawiya Syasneh spray-painted a simple message on a schoolhouse wall: "It's your turn, doctor."[25] In other words, it was the eye-doctor Assad's turn to be overthrown as president.

The Mukhabarat, Syria's fearsome secret police, wasted no time responding to this audacity. At 4 a.m., agents raided the homes of Syasneh and fourteen other students between the ages of ten and fifteen. The youths were arrested and swept away to a detention facility in handcuffs. For two weeks Assad's henchmen subjected them to all sorts of torture and abuse. Some were sprayed with insecticide and set on fire. Some were shocked with electric cables while being doused in a shower. Others were whipped or had their fingernails pulled out. When the boys' fathers showed up to find out what happened, they were told, "Forget those children; go home and make some more. If you can't manage, send us your women and we'll make more for you."[26]

When the battered schoolboys were finally released to their families—including the body of one boy who had been killed in detention—the people of Daraa took to the streets in protest. Assad's police had crossed a line in Syria's tribal society, where daily life is rooted in family loyalty and honor. Every parent knew that the young victims could be their own children. "When the people saw the blood, they went crazy," recalls Ibrahim, a relative of one of the arrested boys. "We all belong to tribes and big families and for us blood is a very, very serious issue."[27] Yet Assad's forces responded to the emotional protests with bullets and tear gas. Security police kept ambulances from carrying the injured to hospitals.

The violence quickly escalated into a nationwide uprising. On March 15, dubbed the Syrian Day of Rage, crowds poured into the streets to express their anger and frustration. They demanded

Smuggling Out Images of War Crimes

Often the relatives of prisoners who disappeared inside Syria's prisons and detention centers were left wondering what had happened to their vanished kin. Beginning in 2012 and 2013, an army photographer for Assad's regime took steps to provide answers, however grim. The photographer, code-named Caesar, used his camera to record deaths in military prisons. As he saw increasing evidence of torture and starvation in the corpses of young prisoners, he turned against the Assad regime in disgust. As he recalled, "When I would take photographs, I would think, how can this government be capable of doing this to its own people?" He began to smuggle the images out of Syria on computer discs and thumb drives. By August 2013, when he fled the country, he had released 53,275 photos to the world. Confronted with the photos, victims' family members wavered between gratitude for knowing the truth and horror at the corpses' battered condition. Assad himself dismissed the photos as allegations without evidence.

In 2020, as the United States readied tougher sanctions against Assad's Syria, the photographs were once more in the news. They provided mute testimony to Assad's crimes. The sanctions law passed by Congress bore Caesar's name in tribute.

Quoted in Scott Pelley, "The Evidence of Syrian President Bashar Assad and His Regime's Legacy of War Crimes," CBS News, July 11, 2021. www.cbsnews.com.

that Assad step down in favor of a new government that would rein in the secret police and institute long-needed reforms. Once again, Assad turned to deadly violence. More than one hundred protesters were gunned down across the country. The day after the massacres, security troops showed up at the victims' funerals and fired on the crowds of mourners. On March 23, special forces commanded by Assad's brother stormed the Omari Mosque, which had become a gathering place for protesters. Five people were killed with stun grenades and gunfire, including a doctor who was treating the injured. The powder keg that Syria had become finally exploded into war.

Chemical Attacks and Carpet-Bombing

Armed skirmishes between government troops and rebel militias broke out across Syria. By July 2012, the fighting had become so widespread that the Red Cross declared the situation a full-blown civil war. Assad showed he was prepared to use any tactics to put down the rebellion. Early on the morning of August 21, 2013, his troops fired rockets containing the nerve gas sarin into the rebel-controlled Ghouta district of Damascus, the capital city. Within minutes, loudspeakers in the area blared urgent warnings for residents to flee. The air filled with smoke and an odor of vinegar and rotten eggs, as people wandered into the street, choking and coughing, some foaming at the mouth. Um Hassan scrambled to escape with her four children. "As we were trying to [leave], I could see people coming out of their homes but they would fall down," recalls Hassan. "We tried to help some of them but they died before we got them to the hospital."[28] In all, about fourteen hundred civilians, mostly women and children, lost their lives in the attack.

The chemical attack on Ghouta was hardly an isolated incident. A 2019 report from the Berlin-based Global Public Policy Institute found that Assad's troops and pro-Assad militias had carried out more than three hundred chemical attacks in the years since Ghouta. These attacks came after Syria had agreed, in talks

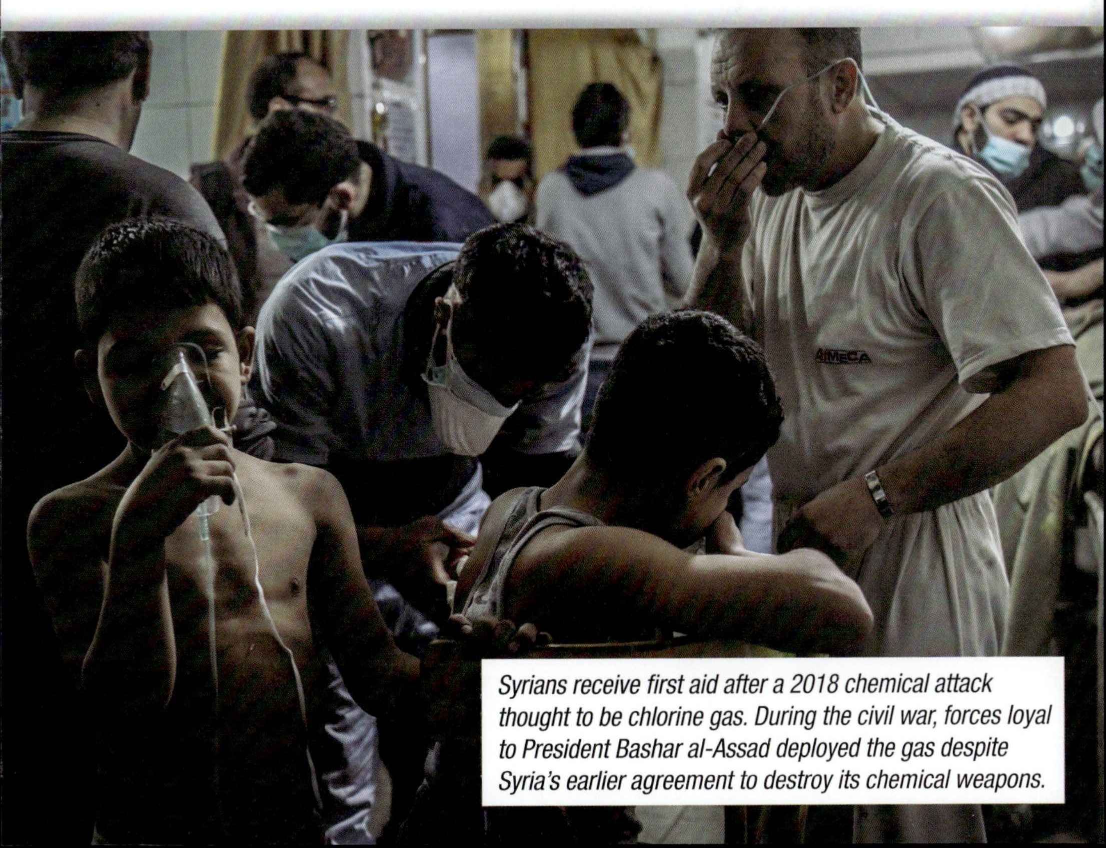

Syrians receive first aid after a 2018 chemical attack thought to be chlorine gas. During the civil war, forces loyal to President Bashar al-Assad deployed the gas despite Syria's earlier agreement to destroy its chemical weapons.

with the United States brokered by Russia, to destroy its cache of chemical weapons. However, in later attacks, Assad's forces used chlorine gas instead of sarin. Because chlorine has peaceful uses, such as in water purification, Assad claimed that its ban had not been part of the deal.

Immediately after the Ghouta attack, calls rang out worldwide for the ICC to prosecute Assad for war crimes. But Syria, along with several other countries, including the United States, had refused to ratify the ICC treaty. Assad was able to ignore any ICC indictment, and the court lacked the means to arrest him. More important to Assad was wiping out the rebellion. "Bashar knows that if he loses this struggle, he's dead," said Joshua Landis, a Syria expert at the University of Oklahoma in Norman, "so some threats of possible international charges at some point in the future aren't his first concern right now."[29]

Another potential war crime was Assad's massive bombing attack on the rebel stronghold in Aleppo, Syria's second-largest city. The attack targeted an area with more than three hundred thousand civilians. Government forces resorted to carpet bombing, or indiscriminate bombing and shelling without regard to the lives of noncombatants. Assad's planes, with help from aircraft flown by Syria's Russian allies, bombed hospitals, restaurants, schools, and homes. They also dropped barrel bombs—crude weapons made of oil barrels or fuel tanks and packed with fuel, explosives, nails, and metal fragments to inflict maximum harm. In one of the worst weeks of carnage, more than one hundred children were killed in bombing strikes. Assad's commanders not only aimed to clear out the rebel militias in Aleppo and other cities, but they also sought to terrorize civilians into rethinking their support for the resistance. "There were bombs and blood everywhere, and you sleep to and wake up by

"Bashar [Assad] knows that if he loses this struggle, he's dead, so some threats of possible international charges at some point in the future aren't his first concern right now."[29]

—Joshua Landis, a Syria expert at the University of Oklahoma

In 2015 rescue workers carry the body of a man who was injured in a reported barrel-bomb attack on Aleppo. The attack by Syrian government forces terrorized and killed many residents.

the sounds of military jets flying over your head and then sounds of air strikes," recalls Ahmad al-Khatib, a native of Aleppo who somehow survived the bombing raids. "Houses were shaking, children were crying and we were all waiting for death."[30]

By the end of 2017, Assad's regime had rained down more than seventy thousand barrel bombs on its own people. Besides bombing many neighborhoods into rubble, government forces also used starvation tactics, deliberately keeping food from reaching those trapped by the fighting.

Cautious Hopes for Prosecution

Although Bashar al-Assad has largely regained control of Syria, the disruptions of civil war continue to plague the region. According to a December 2022 report by the Global Centre for the Responsibility to Protect, at least 580,000 people have died in the war. The fighting has forced 13 million Syrians to abandon their homes, with 6.7 million having fled the nation altogether. Syrian refugees have sought asylum in 130 countries worldwide, but most have settled in neighboring countries such as Turkey, Lebanon, Jordan, Iraq, and Egypt. Among these refugees are scores of eyewitnesses to torture, rape, and murder committed by the Assad regime and its roving militias. It was the brave testimony of Syrian refugees in Germany that enabled the former prison director Anwar Raslan to be brought to justice.

Documentary evidence of war crimes in Syria—the type used to prosecute the Nuremberg defendants—can be difficult to obtain. Most of it has been lost in the war zone. Today, however, officials in the United States and elsewhere cautiously hold out hope that more prosecutions are coming. The Independent Commission for International Justice and Accountability claims to have smuggled out of Syria more than nine hundred thousand government documents that could legally implicate Assad and his lieutenants. Stephen Rapp, a former US ambassador who heads the commission, has experience prosecuting war crimes in Rwanda

Testifying to Syrian War Crimes Despite Threats

Lying awake in a hotel bedroom, Ruham Hawash could not stop thinking about her court appearance the next day. She was scheduled to testify against Anwar Raslan, the Syrian colonel who had overseen her torture and abuse in a Damascus prison nearly a decade earlier. The filth and stench of her prison cell came back to her, as did the fear she had experienced. She knew her testimony would mark her as a target of Assad's secret police, even in Koblenz, Germany, where the trial was being held. Other Syrian refugees had received threats to themselves or their family members should they not heed the warnings to stay silent. But Hawash refused to be intimidated.

On July 21, 2021, Hawash took the stand. She recounted for the court the beatings and electric shocks she had suffered at the hands of Raslan's prison guards. She almost felt embarrassed to focus on her two months of detention, compared to what others had endured inside those walls. In the end, however, her testimony helped convict a war criminal. The verdict gave her a sense of closure. "I can leave it here," she said. "I can start something new."

Quoted in Alia Malek, "How a Syrian War Criminal Was Brought to Justice—in Germany," *New York Times*, January 25, 2022. www.nytimes.com.

and Sierra Leone. Rapp notes that the papers reveal Assad's scheme to imprison, torture, and murder his regime's opponents. "I mean, this is a top down, organized effort," says Rapp. "There are documents with his name on it. Clearly he organizes this strategy. Then we see orders down through the system to pick people up. . . . We see reports back about well, we've got a real problem here, there are too many corpses stacking up."[31]

Victims of Assad's brutality keep pressing for groups such as Rapp's to investigate and prosecute Syrian war crimes and crimes against humanity. But Assad and his officials rarely travel outside Syria and then only to countries that they know will not arrest them. Assad's visit to Dubai in March 2022 marked his first trip to an Arab nation since the start of Syria's civil war. Until Assad's regime is toppled, it seems unlikely that he or his top officials will answer for their crimes in a court of law.

> **"I mean, this is a top down, organized effort. There are documents with [Assad's] name on it. Clearly he organizes this strategy. Then we see orders down through the system to pick people up. . . . We see reports back about well, we've got a real problem here, there are too many corpses stacking up."[31]**
>
> —Stephen Rapp, head of the Independent Commission for International Justice and Accountability

CHAPTER FIVE

Documenting War Crimes in Ukraine

On March 17, 2023, the ICC issued an arrest warrant for Russian president Vladimir Putin for alleged war crimes in Russia's invasion of Ukraine. It was the first time the leader of a nuclear superpower had been charged in this way. Putin, along with a senior Kremlin official, was accused of illegally deporting children from Russian-occupied areas in eastern Ukraine. The second warrant named Maria Lvova-Belova, who serves as Putin's commissioner for children's rights. Thousands of children have been seized by force in Ukraine, transferred to Russia, handed over for adoption to Russian parents, and prevented from contacting loved ones back home. Some have been placed in reeducation camps, to be filled with pro-Russian propaganda.

Lvova-Belova, a longtime advocate for children's rights in Russia, claims that the relocations were undertaken for the children's safety and well-being. But officials in the United States compared Putin's child abductions to Nazi resettlement efforts during World War II. "Separating [children] from their families and then having them adopted by Russians; this is in and of itself, horrific," asserts US secretary of state Antony Blinken. "It also speaks to the fact that President Putin has been trying from day one to erase Ukraine's identity, to erase its future."[32]

Contempt for the World's Standards

Human rights activists worldwide hailed the ICC's action, while analysts were quick to point out there was little chance of arresting Putin or bringing him to trial. Officials in Moscow scoffed at the charges. They also noted that Russia has never signed on to the Rome Statute and does not recognize the ICC's authority. Still, the warrant could create difficulties for Putin. He could be risking arrest if he travels to one of the 123 countries that do participate in the ICC treaty. In theory, that closes off two-thirds of the globe. Even countries that reject the ICC's authority might feel pressured to apprehend a potential war criminal. "Putin is unlikely to leave his destiny to the roll of the dice in a foreign court," says CNN analyst Nic Robertson, "so his world is smaller, even, than the ICC hold-out nations. So regardless of Kremlin spin Putin's ego is dented."[33]

> "Separating [children] from their families and then having them adopted by Russians; this is in and of itself, horrific. It also speaks to the fact that President Putin has been trying from day one to erase Ukraine's identity, to erase its future."[32]
>
> —Anthony Blinken, US secretary of state

Putin has repeatedly shown contempt for the world's standards of civilized behavior. He reacted to the ICC's arrest warrant by traveling to Crimea, the southern peninsula of Ukraine that Russia had annexed in 2014. That annexation began a series of assaults on Ukraine's sovereignty. It culminated in February 2022 with a full-scale invasion of Ukraine. With shocking suddenness, Europe was faced with a nuclear superpower on the march.

A Lawless and Brutal Invasion

From the outset, Putin left no doubt that rules of war would not deter his attempted takeover. Immediately upon invading Ukraine, Russian troops began shelling cities in the country's north, south, and center. The barrage prevented trapped civilians from evacuating. Shelling also destroyed vital infrastructure such as electricity, heating, telecommunications, and water. Cluster bombs—banned under international law—released smaller explosives designed to kill and maim both enemy troops and civilians. The attacks on densely populated areas in Kyiv, Kharkiv, Lviv, and Odessa, including persistent rocket attacks, showed that Putin's goal was to terrorize the populace and weaken its will to resist.

Ukraine's surprising success in repelling the invaders, especially around the capital of Kyiv, seemed to infuriate Putin and his generals. The withdrawal of Russian forces led to more concentrated attacks elsewhere. For example, in Dnipro, southeast of Kyiv, Russian missiles struck apartment buildings and business districts, including a bus station, a car repair shop, and a power plant. Neighborhoods were reduced to rubble within hours. Experts in international law noted that if the attacks deliberately targeted civilians, they certainly qualified as war crimes. "Even where

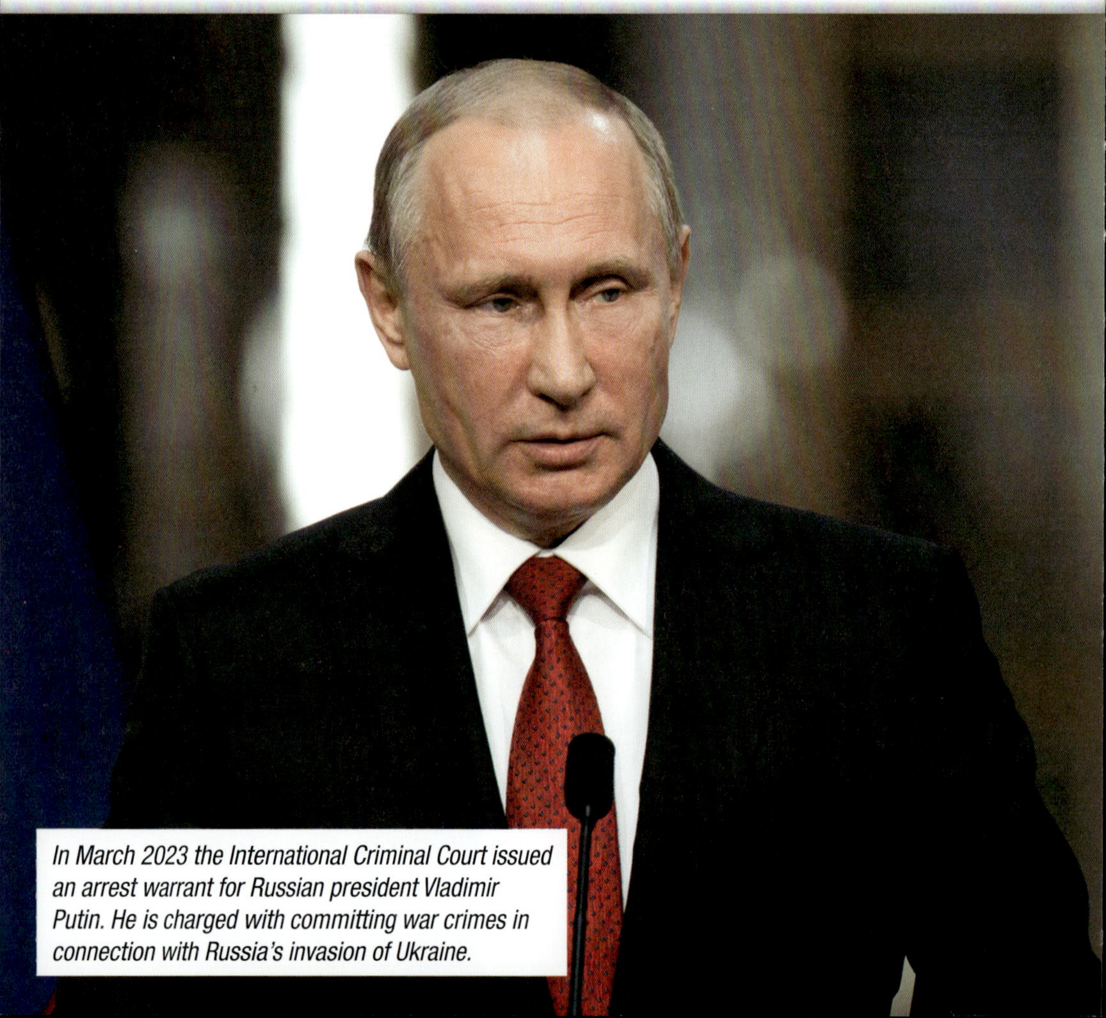

In March 2023 the International Criminal Court issued an arrest warrant for Russian president Vladimir Putin. He is charged with committing war crimes in connection with Russia's invasion of Ukraine.

Putin's History of War Atrocities

Veteran journalists note that the relentless shelling and attacks on civilians are nothing new for Putin. As prime minister in 1999, he authorized a carpet bombing attack on the Chechen city of Grozny that led the UN to call it the most destroyed city on the planet. There were also widespread reports of Russian troops committing rape, torture, arson, and other crimes in their war in Chechnya. In 2015 Putin repeated that playbook in Syria, bombing the rebel-held city of Aleppo to assist his ally Assad. The Russian bombardment of Aleppo, including deliberate attacks on medical centers and residential areas, continued for four years.

The similarities to the 2022 assault on Ukraine have led many Syrians to identify with Ukrainians. Ismail al-Abdullah witnessed Putin's atrocities firsthand as part of a rescue group in Aleppo. He saw hospitals and schools demolished by Russia's indiscriminate bombing attacks. "What happened in Syria is like a lesson for the world that if they did something in the first place to help the Syrian people to stop Russia, maybe this would not be happening," says Abdullah. "Russia would have stopped in the first place in Syria and would not have the courage to invade Ukraine."

Quoted in Jomana Karadsheh, "Syrians Are Watching in Horror as Putin Deploys the Aleppo Playbook in Ukraine," CNN, March 18, 2022. www.cnn.com.

a military target exists," says David Scheffer, the US ambassador-at-large for war crimes issues, "using disproportionate force while knowing that the strike will likely cause death or injury to civilians or damage to civilian structures is a war crime."[34]

Even more disturbing were images from the village of Bucha, just outside Kyiv, where Russian troops massacred townspeople as they withdrew in April 2022. Social media carried chilling images of victims lying dead in the streets or stuffed into drainpipes. Many of the villagers, their hands tied behind them, had been dispatched with a gunshot to the head. As Kyiv's mayor, Vitali Klitschko, said, "What happened in Bucha and other suburbs of Kyiv can only be described as genocide."[35] Later research revealed that it was indeed a so-called cleansing operation to remove opponents of the invasion.

> **"What happened in Bucha and other suburbs of Kyiv can only be described as genocide."[35]**
>
> **—Vitali Klitschko, mayor of Kyiv, Ukraine**

As fighting continues, Ukrainian officials are trying to document war crimes committed by Russia. In 2022 in the town of Bucha, burned human remains are placed in body bags and preserved as evidence of Russian war crimes.

Amassing Evidence of Russian War Crimes

Ukrainians have scrambled to collect evidence of war crimes from the start of Russia's invasion. The day after Russian troops crossed the border, Ukrainian foreign minister Dmytro Kuleba tweeted his intention to collect details of Russian war crimes, including video of missile strikes on an orphanage and a kindergarten. He aimed to send evidence directly to The Hague and the ICC. Indeed, the ICC opened an investigation into possible war crimes on February 28, just days after the invasion.

By March 2023, a little over a year after the war began, Ukrainians claimed to have gathered evidence of more than seventy-five thousand war crimes committed by Russian forces. Ukraine has mounted a nationwide effort to document war crimes in hopes that one day the evidence can be used in an international tribunal like Nuremberg or the Balkan trials in the Hague. The mind-numbing volume of alleged crimes makes the effort especially difficult. Experts warn that it could take years, even decades, to assemble cases for prosecution and bring the perpetrators to justice.

Nonetheless, fueled by outrage at Putin's ongoing slaughter, plenty of individuals and groups have joined the investigations. More than thirty nonprofit groups and nongovernmental organizations (NGOs) have joined an alliance called the Ukraine 5AM Coalition, which seeks to give victims of Russia's aggression a chance to speak out. Some of the groups have been gathering evidence against Russian forces since 2014 and the illegal takeover of Crimea. Several of the NGOs have set up hotlines for eyewitness reports and tips about possible war crimes. Ukrainian investigators have worked with NGO personnel on how to identify prosecutable war crimes.

NGOs have also used their contacts to find journalists and human rights activists who have been imprisoned in Russian-controlled regions of Ukraine. Olha Skrynyk of the Crimean Human Rights Group notes that they have identified 110 people illegally held in an internment camp in Simferopol, the second-largest city in Russian-occupied Crimea. "But the possibilities of locating these people and monitoring their conditions are severely limited," she says, adding that Russia refuses to "recognize these prisoners as prisoners of war, which makes their release practically impossible."[36]

NGOs and outside groups are also working with prosecuting authorities to ensure evidence of war crimes is trustworthy. Apps to create deepfake photos or videos, which are widely available now, can be used to falsify images. Russian apologists often use this fact to question whether images are authentic. To guard against deepfakes, the International Bar Association has developed a mobile app called Eye Witness to Atrocities. The app ensures that photos or videos are genuine by logging the precise coordinates of their recording location. The data is then uploaded to a secure server for safekeeping.

Obtaining the Most Effective Kinds of Evidence

Since the invasion, Ukrainian sources have amassed thousands of hours of cell phone video and hundreds of thousands of photos to document alleged Russian war crimes. However, experts in international law say videos and photos of dead civilians or neighborhoods reduced to rubble are not necessarily the best evidence in prosecuting war crimes. "There is some pretty nasty-looking stuff which I suspect amounts to a crime, but we don't know for certain," explains Bill Wiley, founder and executive director of the Commission for International Justice and Accountability. "It is painfully difficult building cases like this."[37] Such images, says Wiley, do not answer the key question of intent. In other words, who gave the orders that led to the strikes? And did the strikes deliberately target civilians or safe areas? Soldiers can always claim that munitions veered off target, that victims were caught in a cross fire, or that a questionable strike came in response to enemy fire. Determining the truth requires evidence that connects soldiers to their commanders.

Some of the most useful evidence of war crimes comes from intercepted messages. Radio intercepts can reveal where orders came from and how explicit they were in describing the tactics to

Helping the Victims of Sexual Assault in Ukraine

Sexual assault is among the most brutal of the war crimes Russian troops have committed in Ukraine. Several hundred sex-related crimes, such as rape, gang rape, castration, and forced nudity have been reported. Russian soldiers use sexual violence to terrorize civilians and leave them with a feeling of hopelessness. Ukraine's First Lady, Olena Zelenska, has warned that sexual assault has become just another weapon in the invaders' arsenal.

Victims of sexual violence often are haunted by shame and feel reluctant to talk about what happened. Some become depressed and suicidal. An international group called the Global Survivors Fund for Survivors of Conflict-Related Sexual Violence has joined with the Ukrainian government to provide medical and psychological support for these victims. Efforts are made to find them new homes in safer areas. The group also helps victims document their assault while remaining mindful of the trauma involved in reliving the event. "It is difficult to fully confirm sexual violence because it's often the type of case where victims don't want to speak publicly," explains Matilda Bogner, head of a UN investigating team, "and they're often not in safe areas where it feels safe for them to speak out, or where they have received the services that they need."

Quoted in Laurel Wamsley, "Rape Has Reportedly Become a Weapon in Ukraine. Finding Justice May Be Difficult," NPR, April 30, 2022. www.npr.org.

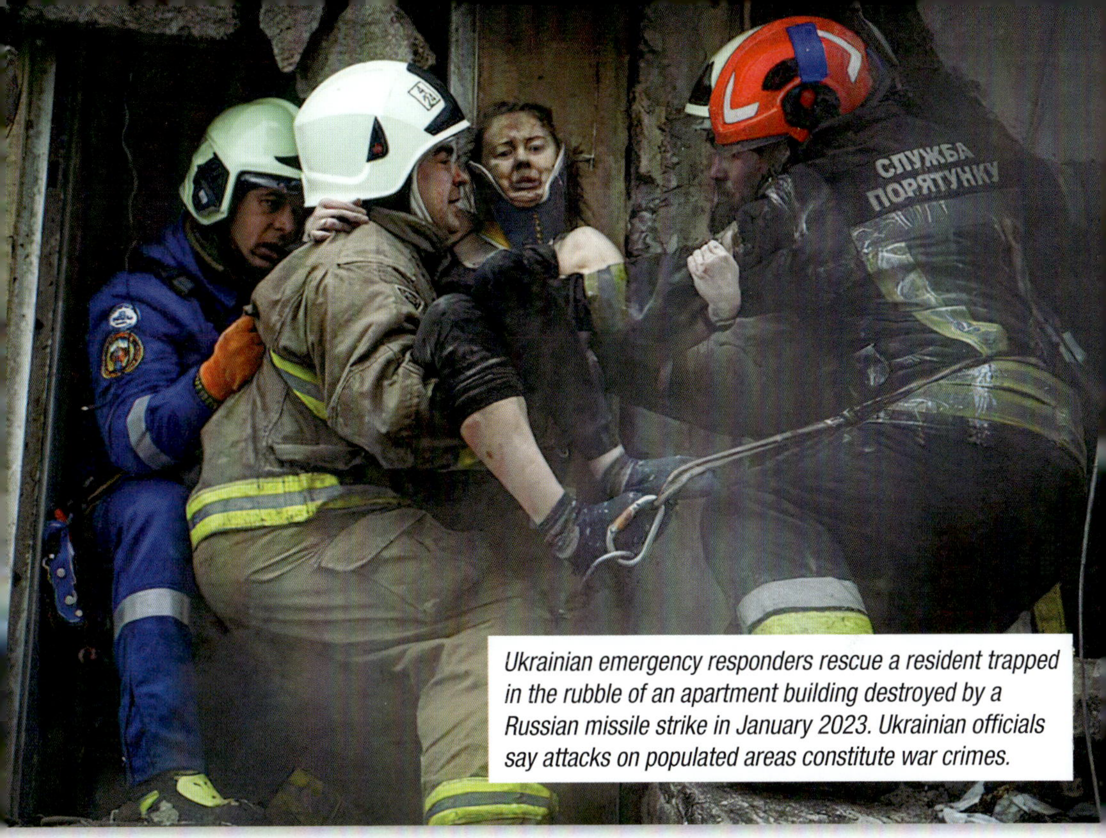

Ukrainian emergency responders rescue a resident trapped in the rubble of an apartment building destroyed by a Russian missile strike in January 2023. Ukrainian officials say attacks on populated areas constitute war crimes.

be deployed. This can enable investigators to track responsibility up the chain of command. For example, Russia's denials about committing the atrocities in Bucha have been challenged by German intelligence. German agents intercepted radio chatter in which a Russian officer matter-of-factly gives precise instructions: "Firstly you question the soldier, then you shoot them."[38] Ukrainian sleuths have managed to intercept radio communications between Russian units on the battlefield. In one recording, the head of an artillery unit is heard to say, "Remove the first military property from the town, then cover the town with artillery fire."[39] Ordering such a concerted attack on civilians could certainly lead to a war crimes conviction. Volunteer radio interceptors in Ukraine say they often listen in as Russian soldiers almost blindly direct the firing of mortars and artillery toward populated areas.

Valuable evidence of war crimes also may be found in the pockets of dead or captured soldiers. Wiley calls this material "pocket debris."[40] It can include cell phones, battlefield maps, code books, handwritten notes, and step-by-step instructions from commanders. Cell phones, which are frequently carried in combat despite being in violation of Russian military rules, are especially valuable. They provide tracking of a unit's movements and photos of others in the group. By offering clues about who ordered what, such "debris" is held in high regard by prosecutors.

Thoroughly Documented War Crimes

Russia's war crimes in Ukraine are some of the most thoroughly documented in history. Social media contains thousands of examples in photos, videos, and interviews with victims. To an unprecedented degree, Ukrainians have set out to document atrocities and crimes against humanity from the war's beginning. Potential war crimes include murders, kidnappings, indiscriminate bombing of civilian areas, and sexual assaults. The ICC's indictment of Putin for war crimes involving the illegal transport of orphans demonstrates the global community's determination to hold him personally responsible.

For all the challenges of documenting Russian war crimes, many experts believe the huge effort will someday produce the desired results. Stephen Rapp, head of the Independent Commission for International Justice and Accountability, says tracing the chain of responsibility from the battlefield to Putin should be easier in Ukraine than it would be in most conflicts. As Rapp observes, "Very little is going to happen in this theater on the Russian side that would not be traceable right up the chain of command, to the top of the Russian state."[41]

"Very little is going to happen in this theater on the Russian side that would not be traceable right up the chain of command, to the top of the Russian state."[41]

—Stephen Rapp, head of the Independent Commission for International Justice and Accountability

SOURCE NOTES

Introduction: A Test for War Crimes Trials in Ukraine

1. Quoted in Pavel Polityuk, "Russian Soldier Jailed for Life in First War Crimes Trial of Ukraine War," Reuters, May 23, 2022. www.reuters.com.
2. Quoted in Alice Speri, "The Mother Crime: Will Putin Face Prosecution for the Crime of Aggression in Ukraine?," *The Intercept,* October 8, 2022. www.theintercept.com.
3. Quoted in Brit McCandless Farmer, "How Bellingcat Is Using TikTok to Investigate the War in Ukraine," CBS News, August 21, 2022. www.cbsnews.com.

Chapter One: The Geneva Conventions and the Laws of Modern Warfare

4. Quoted in Human Rights Watch, "Video Shows Azerbaijan Forces Executing Armenian POWs," October 14, 2022. www.hrw.org.
5. Quoted in Dave Roos, "How the Shocking Use of Gas in World War I Led Nations to Ban It," History, May 17, 2021. www.history.com.
6. Quoted in Roos, "How the Shocking Use of Gas in World War I Led Nations to Ban It."
7. Quoted in National WWII Museum, "Crimes Against Humanity and the Development of International Law," September 15, 2021. www.nationalww2museum.org.
8. Quoted in United States Holocaust Memorial Museum, "Coining a Word and Championing a Cause: The Story of Raphael Lemkin," Holocaust Encyclopedia. https://encyclopedia.ushmn.org.
9. International Committee of the Red Cross, "The Geneva Conventions of 1949 and Their Additional Protocols." www.icrc.org.

Chapter Two: The Nuremberg Trials

10. Jerry Bergman, "The Failed Attempt to Prove Jewish Inferiority by a Skeleton Collection," *Answers Research Journal,* December 16, 2020. https://assets.answersingenesis.org.
11. Quoted in Avalon Project, "International Conference on Military Trials: London, 1945. Memorandum to President Roosevelt from the Secretaries of State and War and the Attorney General, January 22, 1945," Yale Law School. http://avalon.law.yale.edu.

12. Quoted in National WWII Museum, "The Nuremberg Trial and Its Legacy," November 17, 2020. www.nationalww2museum.org.
13. Quoted in National WWII Museum, "'The Grave Responsibility of Justice': Justice Robert H. Jackson's Opening Statement at Nuremberg," November 20, 2020. www.nationalww2museum.org.
14. Quoted in Douglas O. Linder, "Defendants in the Major War Figures Trial," Famous Trials. https://famous-trials.com.
15. Quoted in Douglas O. Linder, "Excerpts of the Testimony of Hermann Goering 3," Famous Trials, https://famous-trials.com.
16. Quoted in Christopher Klein, "10 Things You May Not Know About the Nuremberg Trials," History, September 29, 2021. www.history.com.
17. Quoted in Audiovisual Library of International Law, "Affirmation of the Principles of International Law Recognized by the Charter of the Nürnberg Tribunal—General Assembly Resolution 95," United Nations. https://legal.un.org.

Chapter Three: Prosecuting War Crimes in the Former Yugoslavia

18. Quoted in Adam Ferrise, "Feds Arrest Parma Heights Man Accused of Committing War Crimes as Part of Yugoslavian People's Army, Officials Say," Cleveland.com, January 26, 2023. www.cleveland.com.
19. Quoted in *New York Times,* "Srebrenica: A U.N. 'Safe Haven' That Soon Was Not," October 29, 1995. https://timesmachine.nytimes.com.
20. Quoted in Julian Borger, "The Manhunt," International Bar Association. www.ibanet.org.
21. Quoted in Julian Borger, "The Hunt for the Former Yugoslavia's War Criminals: Mission Accomplished," *The Guardian,* August 3, 2011. www.theguardian.com.
22. Peter Beaumont, "Slobodan Milosevic Dies Alone with History Still Demanding Justice," *The Guardian,* March 11, 2006. www.theguardian.com.
23. Quoted in Marlise Simons, "Yugoslavia Tribunal Leaves Rich Legacy, but 'Immense' Challenges Remain," *New York Times,* December 23, 2017. www.nytimes.com.

Chapter Four: Confronting War Crimes in Syria

24. Quoted in *New York Times,* "Syria War Crimes Verdict: Former Syrian Colonel Guilty in War Crimes Trial in Germany," January 13, 2022. www.nytimes.com.
25. Quoted in Benjamin Nweke, "The Boy Who Started the Syrian Civil War," Medium, May 27, 2021. www.medium.com.
26. Quoted in Nweke, "The Boy Who Started the Syrian Civil War."

27. Quoted in CBS News, "How Schoolboys Began the Syrian Revolution," April 26, 2011. www.cbsnews.com.
28. Quoted in Mona Mahmood and Martin Chulov, "Syrian Eyewitness Accounts of Alleged Chemical Weapons Attack in Damascus," *The Guardian,* August 22, 2013. www.theguardian.com.
29. Quoted in Howard LaFranchi, "Is Assad Scared of a War Crimes Trial? Assault on Homs Suggests Not," *Christian Science Monitor,* March 1, 2012. www.csmonitor.com.
30. Quoted in Shawn Yuan, "Syrians Recount Horror Under Russian Air Attacks," Al Jazeera, March 5, 2022. www.aljazeera.com.
31. Quoted in Scott Pelley, "The Evidence of Syrian President Bashar Assad and His Regime's Legacy of War Crimes," CBS News, July 11, 2021. www.cbsnews.com.

Chapter Five: Documenting War Crimes in Ukraine

32. Quoted in Josh Meyer, "Ukrainian Children Taken to Russia Brings Back Fear, Memories of a Similar Nazi Effort," *USA Today,* March 17, 2023. www.usatoday.com.
33. Nic Robertson, "Putin's World Just Got a Lot Smaller with the ICC's Arrest Warrant," CNN, March 19, 2023. www.cnn.com.
34. Quoted in William M. Arkin, "War Crimes Investigation: Is Putin Targeting Civilians in Ukraine?," *Newsweek,* August 1, 2022. www.newsweek.com.
35. Quoted in Associated Press, "Kyiv Mayor Says Russian Attacks in Bucha Are 'Genocide,'" *Times of Israel,* April 3, 2022. www.timesofisrael.com.
36. Quoted in Igor Burdyga, "Ukraine: NGOs Help Prosecutors Document Russian War Crimes," Deutsche Welle, March 23, 2023. www.dw.com.
37. Quoted in Vivienne Walt, "Building a War Crimes Case Against Putin Is Harder than You Think," *Time,* March 10, 2022. www.time.com.
38. Quoted in Kate Connolly and Bethan McKernan, "Russian Soldiers 'Discussed Killing Civilians' in Ukraine in Radio Intercepts," *The Guardian,* April 7, 2022. www.theguardian.com.
39. Quoted in Katya Bandouil and Richard Hall, "'Cover the Town with Artillery Fire': Online Sleuths Are Intercepting Russian Radio Communications and Revealing Potential War Crimes," *The Independent* (London), March 3, 2022. www.independent.co.uk.
40. Quoted in Walt, "Building a War Crimes Case Against Putin Is Harder than You Think."
41. Quoted in Walt, "Building a War Crimes Case Against Putin Is Harder than You Think."

FOR FURTHER RESEARCH

Books

Vladimir Dzuro, *The Investigator: Demons of the Balkan War.* Sterling, VA: Potomac, 2019.

Luke Harding, *Invasion: The Inside Story of Russia's Bloody War and Ukraine's Fight for Survival.* New York: Vintage, 2022.

Airey Neave, *Nuremberg: A Personal Record of the Trial of the Major Nazi War Criminals.* Hull, UK: Biteback, 2021.

Ann Petrila and Hasan Hasanovic, *Voices from Srebrenica: Survivor Narratives of the Bosnian Genocide.* Jefferson, NC: McFarland, 2020.

Dan Plesch, *Human Rights After Hitler: The Lost History of Prosecuting Axis War Crimes.* Washington, DC: Georgetown University Press, 2017.

Internet Sources

Masha Gessen, "The Prosecution of Russian War Crimes in Ukraine," *New Yorker,* August 1, 2022. www.newyorker.com.

Laurin-Whitney Gottbrath, "What Counts as a War Crime and Why They're So Hard to Prosecute," Axios, March 23, 2022. www.axios.com.

National WWII Museum, "The Nuremberg Trials." www.nationalww2museum.org.

Marlise Simons and Marc Santora, "Tribunal Convicts Former Serbian Officials of Crimes in Balkan Wars," *New York Times,* June 30, 2021. www.nytimes.

Ali Haj Suleiman and Kareem Chehayeb, "Syrians Seek Justice for War Atrocities 11 Years After Uprising," Al Jazeera, March 15, 2022. www.aljazeera.com.

Zachary B. Wolf, "How War Crimes Prosecutions Work," CNN, March 17, 2023. www.cnn.com.

Organizations and Websites

Center for Justice and Accountability (CJA)
www.cja.org
The CJA is the leading nongovernmental organization that brings civil and criminal cases against individual human rights abusers for

war crimes. The CJA's website includes stories about the organization's current cases and investigations.

Hoover Institution
www.hoover.org
The Hoover Institution is a public policy think tank that seeks to improve the human condition by advancing ideas that promote economic opportunity and prosperity while securing and safeguarding peace for America and all nations. Its website features several analyses about war crimes and related issues, including "War Crimes in Ukraine: The Pursuit of International Justice."

Human Rights Watch (HRW)
www.hrw.org
HRW defends the rights of people in close to one hundred countries worldwide, spotlighting abuses and bringing perpetrators to justice. Articles on the HRW website include a discussion of the US Congress's Justice for Victims of War Crimes Act and an investigation of child abductions in Ukraine.

International Committee of the Red Cross (ICRC)
www.icrc.org
The International Committee of the Red Cross is an independent, neutral organization ensuring humanitarian protection and assistance for victims of armed conflict and other situations of violence. The ICRC's website features articles about its mission and its current role in helping victims of armed conflict worldwide.

International Criminal Court (ICC)
www.icc-cpi.int
The ICC investigates and, where warranted, tries individuals charged with the gravest crimes of concern to the international community: genocide, war crimes, crimes against humanity, and the crime of aggression. The ICC's website contains stories and information about current trials and investigations for war crimes and trust funds for victims of war crimes.

United States Holocaust Memorial Museum
www.ushmm.org
The United States Holocaust Memorial Museum stands as a living memorial to the Holocaust. It inspires citizens and leaders worldwide to confront hatred, prevent genocide, and promote human dignity. The museum's website includes a comprehensive encyclopedia of the Holocaust and Nazi war crimes during World War II.

INDEX